The Marks Humans Leave

Aden Carroll

Copyright © 2023 by Aden Carroll

All rights reserved.

No portion of this book may be reproduced in any form without written permission from the publisher or author, except as permitted by U.S. copyright law.

Table of Contents

"Wingspans" 1
"Necropolis" 4
"On The Day of Our Divorce Hearing" 6
"The Ruins" 9
"Ode to Death" 11
"Ode to Grief" 12
"Mississippi Alms" 13
"The Rebirth of Kore" 15
"To the Eating of Sins" 18
"Lifeline" 22
"The Prayer of the Lonely" 25
"True North" 27
"Gratify" 29
"Slow Disease" 30
"Ode to Miracles" 33
"The Dark Side of a Meadowlark" 34
"Seed" 35
"2006" 36
"Taste" 37
"It Means Shadow" 40
"Name" 43
"Evanesce" 45
"The Things Unknown" 48
"The Crisis of Captivity" 51

"The Marks Humans Leave" 60
"Declaration of War" 62
"Burning House" 64
"Awakening" 65
"Creation Unseen" 66
"Desolation" 67
"War" 68
"The Road" 71
"Home" 72
"Certain Things" 73
"From Earth" 74

"Wingspans"

On the edge of a river
the earth is ripe for breeding.
The warm brown earth aches to be planted,
to germinate,
to be harvested.

On the edge of a river
surrounded on either side by dry land and dust,
my father built his life,
stone by stone,
flight by flight.

This yellow flight,
steady and sure,
mangled and uncertain,
both created and destroyed him.

This was what he captured and tamed,
what he learned and forgot.

This was what he chose,
and did not choose.
What he loved
and despised.

From the depths of heaven,
the position of clouds,
the wingspans of stratospheres,
the shape of his world appeared.

And it is there that he remains,
the lone observer of such a tragic view.

A sky wrought with war and blood,
fire and terror,
A sky that bore such smoke,
such abandonment,
such abominable weeping.

A realm of birth and light
that poured him libations of sunsets and harvests,
of travels and trains,
of homes and children,

The same radiant empyrean shining in cathedral gold
that offered so much,
but in return took fear,
flesh,
and his brother
as payment.

"Necropolis"

You stand tall and proud and empty.
like an oak tree full of tumors,
bulging at it seam with death and rot.

Hanging from your twisted branches,
the remnants of those who've been conquered,
the flesh of those you have skinned,

They hang spent and loose,
like old coveralls on the line after the wash,

Do you keep them as trophies?
Metals for viewing?
How does it feel to know your daughter rests amongst them?

She will not live there.
She will not stay.
You pitched her out into your graveyard of discarded things,
but I caught her.
and loved her in ways you cannot.

She spent days believing you would pull her from the line.

That hope now lies lifeless in the boneyard of your failure.

Now she sees you as you truly are.

A suit with no man,

A winter coat with nothing underneath,

Like cotton candy, spools of sugar that at the first taste dissolve into nothing.

And that thought both comforts and haunts me.

"On The Day of Our Divorce Hearing"

You stood,
Your arm draped around her shoulder,
In the lobby of the courthouse.
I walked past you both,
Holding fresh docket papers,
The ink still wet,
The remnants of eighteen years of my life
In a manilla file folder
Beneath my arm.

I sat in a harsh wooden chair
With burgundy leather wrapped arms,
My fingers spread out over the lip
Of a mahogany court table,

She snickered at something you said,
And you leaned into her neck whispering "shh."
Then a voice reading pages and pages and pages.
"The marriage is irretrievably broken."
A judge asked, "Is there anything else you need to add, Mrs. Carroll?"

No.
Nothing.
Everything.
Scream.
Cry.
Curse.
Yell.

"No. Nothing."

The scribbling of my name and a date,
A thick black line down the center of my life.

I picked up the beige folder,
Gathered what was left of my life,
And made my way outside.

In the middle of the parking lot,
You caught me
And said, "We both know I didn't love you. You're better off."

So off you two went to our red truck,
And me to our gray jeep.

It's three years later and even that's just a story now.

Lately I don't feel as if I ever lived with you.

But I remember that day,

And how that was likely the most honest thing you had ever told me.

"The Ruins"

In the murky corners
of a new and strange place,
unrestrained by ages of shame,
unkept by demons of my own making,
I find the sullied and dark things
I already knew existed.

I skulk around them,
memorizing their shape and likeness.
I study the composition of things.
I trace the edges of this place with chipped nails, twisted curiosity, and fierce self-doubt.

In my agony,
in the depths of my loneliness,
I find both heaven and hell.

That bleak and broken place
can never be ignored,
can never be forgotten,
because although it broke me
in all the ways that mattered,

I discovered a sinewed backbone that had long been smothered by misuse and frailty.

Despite the depraved reality around me,
despite the rotten forces hiding in plain sight,
I learned the true measure of my creation.

Despite the puppeteer working time and space,
manipulating fact,
molding humans to his liking,
there was more truth buried in those
walls than in any science or religion.

These are the facts that remain.

We are all our own form of destruction.

Our existence is a miraculous and rebellious act of planting our feet

when all we want to do is fall.

"Ode to Death"

In the end
every word you said drew blood.
My thoughts were so full of you
that there was no room for me left.

"Ode to Grief"

I have learned
That when grief comes to visit,
All I can do is say is
"I see you."

I sit down with her,
Hands shaking at the kitchen table,
And bring her a cup of coffee,
Black and bitter just the way she likes it,

I give her room to moan,
To thrash and scream,
To rage and whimper,
I let her say what she needs to say,

Then before sunset,
When it's good and time for company to go,
I ask her to leave.

Because I opened the front door,
Asked her inside,
And let her speak,

I can let her go.

"Mississippi Alms"

Due east atop a hovering expanse of concrete bridge,

That weds one of my homes with another,

The sun rears its radiant head proudly,

Beaming through the breaks in the cable-stayed sides

Like daybreak through wooden slat shutters,

The early morning delta sun takes its time burning its way through the fog

That still desperately clings to the surface of the water,

The river here moves differently,

She isn't bound by the same laws of nature as most,

Her migration is her own,

Her heading is the open sea,

Before queen mother Mississippi meets her beloved brine to the far south,

She releases the remnants of things not meant for her,

The hard and shattered things that she doesn't want to hold any longer,

The river leaves behind the parts of herself that are too heavy,

The portions too thick with the past to keep alongside her,

The accumulated sediment of a thousand years and lifetimes,

And the famished earth graciously accepts this oblation,

The delta plains fervently accept this offering,

Ravenous in their thirst for something of substance,

They bathe themselves the minerals left by what the Mississippi would not carry,

Life is created from this covenant,

From this act of release,

Cattails and cotton,

Swamp rose and soybeans,

Spider lilies and cypress trees,

All progeny of letting go,

A testament to the act of leaving weighty things behind.

"The Rebirth of Kore"

Her fiction was born of ambrosia,

Yet her story is more than crimson currants and golden apples,

Though the spectacle of changing seasons bends to her will,

Her gift was offered through agony,

The endowment of her skill was created from torment and grief,

In her innocent youth she reigned over the beginnings of flowers,

Her tender palm soothed the newborn fawns,

The dark tendrils of her hair blanketed the starkness of winter,

Warming the earth for the sweetness of Spring.

Taken by circumstance and greed,

A marriage bed made of fire and death,

She made a home amongst demons and demise,

And there she waited for millennia,

The maiden of the seasons carved out a place where she could survive,

A small corner she could hide herself,

This girl of sunlight and softness,

The premature queen of the underworld,

The boundaries between choice and capture

Between sacrifice and slavery,

Were scattered amongst what remained of herself,

Blurred by the smog of hunger and blood,

When the smoke of the war cleared

And she came to the end of the world,

The sin which had dragged her beneath the splitting earth,

Was revealed,

The misery of the world dissipated,
And she knew all at once that she was no flower girl,
No gentle wind against the trees,
Her shaking breath was a cry of defiance,
Her shriek was the breaker of chains,

She is the giver of life
And the harbor of death,
She is the queen of hell
And the mother of every woman.

"To the Eating of Sins"

There were so many shards and pieces,
so many little parts,
one million tiny things that accumulated to create me,

Some of these things were dark and sharp and sore,
some were coarse and impenetrable and raw,

I walked a long while carrying all those slivers and fragments,

focusing only on the movement of my feet,

on not letting one of those murky portions of me hit the floor.

I walked many years alone through the crepuscular fog,

holding these jagged parts,

and the weight of another man's sins.

I lived a thousand lifetimes holding onto these black decaying things,

clasping to them like moss on a damp wall,

fastening myself to them like a suit of armor,

clinging to them like the pain of longing,

like a drowning man clutching to emptiness.

It took me years to understand that I was molding those dark and dead things into a capable shield.

After carrying these for a millennium,

my arms began to fail,

my legs to shudder,

and I began to comprehend the full weight of all my separate parts,

Then all at once you were there,
In the midst of sheer chaos,
there you were,
and you smiled at me.

You don't yet know this,
but you saved me.
from my mind,
from my torment,
from myself,
from the idea that I am not
worthy of a love like yours.

You make me question the truths of this universe,
the very fabric of nature,
the gospel of the cosmos itself.

Your aura is made of laughter and kindness,
of patience and consistency.

Caught up in your substance
and without noticing,
I laid them down,
all the broken and damaged pieces
I'd been clinging to for so long,

I laid them down in the light of you.

I laid each one down one by one for you to see,
and you did not run.
The world folded in on itself,
and I realized that dark weight no longer served me.

It was the midafternoon sunlight that changed your eyes
from grey to robin blue.

And now that I that I know you exist,
how can I not love you?

"Lifeline"

I had made peace with contentment many years ago,
In the aftermath of battle,
My body had made a pact with the comfortability of one,
My own hand,
My own eyes,
My own heartbeat,

Sitting in a dark theater beside you,
I felt you without touch,
The air of you settled effortlessly nearby,
And the atmosphere around me altered,
Became something new,
Something thicker and safer,
Something simpler and yet somehow more,

I drew breath but it felt different,
It warmed me from my core,
And set my skin on fire,
I willed myself to breathe,
I prayed you wouldn't see,
The ache in my center,
The heat in my chest,
I begged God to hide from you
The pure elemental want I had to be right here,
Right now,
Next to you,

The intrinsic need for you to be tethered to me,

Then you moved slightly,
Slid your arm against mine,
Lightening against my forearm,
A crash of balmy heat filling my lungs,

Your fingers reached for mine,
Found my frightened and clammy grasp,
And I lost the battle between what I believe to be true
And the axiom of what my soul was whispering,

Your finger traced the inside of my palm,
A balm of Gilead over me,
Calm, warm, and full of stars,
Tenderness mixed with pure wild abandon,
The remedy of an illness I didn't know I had,

You drew a slow line with the pad of your finger over my lifeline,
And I met your gaze,
Those eyes like clouds, full of rain and thunder,
And I felt a thousand heartbreaking days vanish,
A lifetime of war dissipated in the air between your lips and mine,

Your fingers laced between my fingers
And held me there,
And I knew,
All at once,
That nothing would ever be the same for me.

"The Prayer of the Lonely"

You arrived gently,
Seated like you had been here before,
Calm and deliberate,
Like a glass of red wine,
Sip by intoxicating sip,
Sliding past my parched lips,
Tasting of darkness and salt,
Of the mineral sweetness of earth,

The tannin of you invades my tongue,
Creeping into the hollow parts of me,
Finding its' way into the creeks and tributaries,
That have long been asleep,

And all at once,
The world is rotating,
The truth of my existence turns on its axis,
And my view of known things changes,

I'm drowning in a warmth that feels like home.

You feel like stout glass of bourbon,
Strong and thick,
Heating my chest from the inside,
Blurring the edges of my vision.

I send a silent prayer into the atmosphere,
Into the dense smoke around me,
A beggar's plea,
"Let me keep my sight."

"True North"

You arouse me
In the simplest form.
The feel of your scruff against my nails,
The taste of your mouth after you sip whiskey,
Your voice in the morning,
A deep, low growl against my shoulder,

Your words crawl beneath my skin,
Syllable by sweet syllable stretched out beneath the cover of my flesh,
I hide them there where only I can feel them,
A hidden gospel,
Secret scriptures that belong to only me,
An intoxication beyond reason,
You steady me and stir me.

I long to learn the uncharted things,
The portions you keep guarded behind those grey eyes,
To be closer to you,
The most tender and terrifying place I don't yet know,

When I look at you,
My senses shift,
My compass needle turns,
My soul sways,
And that's how I know.

My heart has been on unkind roads.
You feel like a prayer through which God is making it up to me.

"Gratify"

you breathed
hot and fast,
burning God's name
into the side of my neck,

my teeth sank into my bottom lip
begging to draw blood,

i closed my eyes
and whispered a prayer of my own
"please lord,
overlook what i will do to him"

"Slow Disease"

The homosexual young men and the amorous girls in velvet dresses,
the dark eyed widows who suffer from delirious insomnia,
and the young supple wives thirty hours pregnant,
the stinking string of yowling cats that cross the ally in the dark,
like a necklace of throbbing sexual oysters,

They all surround my solitary residence,
like enemies of the state,
like conspirators dressed in black and carrying daggers,
who have exchanged allegiance through long, thick, strange kisses,
full of anonymity and absent of names, ages, and emotion.

The radiant summer in its cathedral gold leads them all
in dark, uniform, melancholy regiments,
made of fat and skinny,
happy and sad couples.

Beneath the elegant east coast trees,
beside the ancient ocean and the moon,
there is a continuous life of trousers and skirts,
a rustle of silk stockings and blouses,
of forced cleavage that shine like eyes,
like ripe red apples,

The little, needy employee after quite a while,

after the weekly tedium,

and the cheap paperback novels read alone in bed,

will seduce his neighbor,

and take her to miserable movies

where the heroes are cops, or passionate princes,

and the heroines are tall and lean and do not speak.

He'll stroke her legs stretched thin with nylon and scented lotions

with his impatient and clammy hands that smell of cigarettes.

The twilights of the seducers and the long sweaty nights of spouses pile up,

like freshly dirtied sheets,

the lunch hours when the young male students

and the young female students

and the priests masturbate,

when the animals copulate in the street as traffic passes by,

and the bees smell of blood

and the flies buzz angrily,

when boy cousins play strangely with their girl cousins,

and the irate doctor looks furiously at the husband of the inexperienced and bruised patient,

when the adulterers who love each other upon beds as lofty and lengthy as ships,

porting in another harbor each night,

having their full of the locals,

I am securely and eternally surrounded by this great respiratory machine,

this entangled forest full of overgrown flowers that stand like mouths and broken teeth,

and black rotting roots shaped like phalli and fingernails,

a forest that smells like cheap cigars and bottom self-whiskey,

and sounds like young girls crying and old men grinning,

I am encompassed by this slow disease,

this reptilian plague

that infects the planet,

leaving nothing in its wake but pieces of promises,

empty vesicles,

dried semen,

and peckish women,

filled to their brim with the infection of sperm and salt,

and so, this is our untimely end,

killed by the very thing that created us.

"Ode to Miracles"

I just left your voice
that deep, husky "goodnight"
still lingering in the air
over my bed,

But I won't let you go just yet
I hold that sound with both hands
cradling it between the palms of my hands
just one more minute,

I want to feel it's heat
against my chest
it's low growl traveling up my neck
whispering to me all the things he might do
to me before sleep.

"The Dark Side of a Meadowlark"

Alone again, sleeping by myself,
Another thought bad for my health,
I've seen it all through someone else,
Another thought bad for myself.

Appreciated, but undisturbed,
I'm serenated by a mockingbird,
That's seldom seen, and never heard,
I'm serenated by a mockingbird,

Disintegrated by the rising sun,
Empty stories just begun,
It's all a form of oblivion,
Empty stories just begun,

So I drive up north to make some noise,
There's just no justice to what he enjoys,
They tell me "boys will be boys," but,
There's just no justice to what he enjoys.

Fight the shadow when it all falls apart,
I am slow to finish, but quick to start.
I am the dark side of a meadowlark.
I am slow to finish but quick to start.

"Seed"

Through the scent of pleasantries appear,
The infallible variables of "x,"
With the slip of the tongue, I disappear,
And the talk resumes of sex,

Dispensable, I listen well,
But careful not to hear,
Invisible, such an easy sell,
But its cost remains unclear,

Of all that I appear to be
Of skin and brain unbound,
A question of identity,
And planets crashing to the ground,

The "sorry" girl so fragrant sweet,
Still occupies a room,
That corner where her ends don't meet,
Will be the color of her doom,

"The story writes itself," they think,
A happy one, indeed.
The shape of her world turns rose pink,
And there sprouts the killing seed.

"2006"

Bruises made. Band-aid.
Ends frayed. Air raid.
Pseudo-renegade. Emotional blockade.
Call a spade a spade.

Infantilize. Sunrise.
Money buys quiet eyes.
Immobilize. Hypnotize.
Absent cries. Finalize.

Me, null and void.
You, overjoyed.
Us, a pair devoid.
I miss the two people we both avoid.

"Taste"

Of false astrologies,
of customs habitual and somewhat gloomy,
poured into the interminable glass of compulsion
and always carried in the right hand,
I have retained a tendency,
a solitary and obsessive taste,
an intensity to hold onto the wheel,
it helps to cushion the inevitable blow.

Of conversations and whispers
as worn out as an old wood and shoestrings,
with the humility of experience and guilt,
with words serving as slaves to unfit masters,
the consistency of stale bread,
of hard water,
and dead weeks,
of swollen and sick letters,

Who can boast of a more solid taste?
Born of this taste was prudence,
and she wraps me in a compact and tight skin
the color of metal,
coiled like a snake.

My scars and scales are born from a slow and long rejection,

and with a single drink,

a solitary swallow,

I can dismiss the day without guilt,

without passion,

as unequal among such other earthly days.

I have lived with a substance of awkward color so long,

it has become the bulk of me,

silent and stoic like an old mother,

a patience as fixed and framed as a church shadow,

or a gathering of bones.

And so I go,

filled with those waters,

purposefully arranged,

falling to sleep in a sad and disinterested attention.

Inside my head,

there is an old air,

dry and resonant,

left behind and motionless,

like a faithful hunger,

like smoke,

It is an element of rest,
a living oil,
a burning ember bursting into hot, red flame.

An essential bird watches over my head,
a constant angel lives in my sword,
that swarthy blade of cynicism and sarcasm,
A cold wind is present in my dreams.
It is fear dressed in loneliness and endless time.

My habitual taste serves only to force the fear into submission,
and soon enough the terror subsides,
and there I force it into a box,
a dismal coat closet inside my brain,
where I keep it,
crammed in like a parachute.

"It Means Shadow"

How silly to think of it,
What pure and formulaic omen,
A definitive kiss and a farewell
To bury the heart,
To yield in the origins of helplessness
And ignorance

What a strange new angel of dreams
That lays upon my sleepy shoulders
For perpetual safety,
It is a futile engagement.

For this new angel
There is only the killing of time,
The planting of seeds,
The germination of questions unnoticed and unwanted,

Perhaps the natural weakness of suspicion
And the anxious worry of things,
Suddenly seeks out permanence,
The problem of eternity,

Perhaps it searches for life in time,
And as we all do,
Its limits on earth,

Perhaps the sin and the ages
Accumulate,
Extending outward from here
Like lunar waves of an ocean newly created,
Like the lands and shores we've so grievously ravaged,

Let what I am,
What you are,
What we have become,
Go on existing,
And ceasing to exist.

May my obedience be born
from such iron conditions
that the color and tremor of death
and war
and births
will not trouble that space within me
that I so stridently try to keep for myself,
my nook of dark things and dried flower petals,

Let what I am, then,
be in some places,
in some times,
an established
and ardent witness,
eagerly insistent upon the verity of the human condition,
that there is little livable space between wanting to believe
and our innate unwillingness to do so.

"Name"

In the depths of a dense summer,
I heard a rustling of sounds,
In the cool shade of a long day,
Like a brown painted horse,
Your name runs past,

Sew me to your skin,
Stitch me to your seams,
And appear to me suddenly
Outside this nocturnal pane of my window,

Flowers of orange and green
Pain me in the wake of your absence,
And because of it,
The fragrance of summer
Inflicts upon me
A moral and delicate sadness,

Now and then,
In "the long run,"
From oblivion to oblivion,
I hold these moments
The cry of the rain,
The howl at the window

The shape of your hand against my face,
All of the honest moments
That the dark and solitary night preserves

Call me home in the apricot evening,
When the crickets sing at dusk,
The world around me grows lavender,
And the tree lines make music.

Bring your substance
Your brown skin,
Your sea storm eyes,
And sit with me.
Sit beside me in the quiet
And let your existence encompass me,
As if you were this place itself,
This spot of green where my life exists.

"Evanesce"

I was seven years old the first time I disappeared.

Lying in my pink chiffon bed listening to the witches and the wolves,

The crickets and giants creeping and moaning outside my window,

I often wondered where I could disappear to,

Where I could hide away from such an overwhelming and impending doom.

Sometimes I thought of hiding beneath the bed,
Behind the door,
Between the coats in the closet,
The familiar places once instinctually remembers when fear grips them,
Or when they find themselves with only a few fleeting moments left to hide
During a game of hide and seek.

But mostly I would imagine myself disappearing altogether.
I'd pull my arm, legs, and feet in so tightly,
My limbs twisting and twirling into a sphere of bone and fear.

I'd imagine the pressure rising,
Becoming so great that my skin would dissolve,
My flesh melting into bone,
My bone into fluid,
My fluid to oxygen.

I'd imagine my body folding into itself,
Onto itself,
Skin into skin,
Until nothing remained,
Only my memory dancing on the wind.

I was seven years old the first time I disappeared.
I didn't know then,
That the act of evanescence,
Would be a skill I employed for the rest of my life.

"The Things Unknown"

Moon beams.
Jet streams.
Bad dreams.
He leaves.
She grieves.

In the beginning there was the word,
The news,
The war,
The way of all flesh,
The inevitable and unbearable price you must pay,

Nothing to be done.

So for the breadth of a river,
A vast and immeasurable ocean,
We stared without speaking.

There was nothing to be said.

The world was already on fire,
Smoldering in its own pregnant notions of entitlement.

Serious.
Delirious.
Imperious.
Weary us.

The things we did not know
Could fill two distant and separate continents,
Each one too close
To notice one another,
And too far away to care,
Relics of an innocent
And unblemished age,
Long since dead.

I have pictured it many times,
That moment so carefully stitched together,
Forming a single word,
Hope
And I wondered how I might ever catch such a thing
One handed,

But it cannot be caught,
Only created,

It must be forged from steel
And optimism,
From want,

And despair,

And so it is that everything that comes of morning,
Undoes itself before nightfall,
The hummingbird returns to the nest,
The rain washes away the unclean byproducts of the day,
The sun sinks away,
Passes out,
Goes dark,
And nothing exists.

Ashes to ashes,
Dust to dust,
Along the way,
Life interrupts.

"The Crisis of Captivity"

It's a sticky topic,
A complicated one too,
A real primordial query,
Look around,
The range spreads,
The differences accumulate,
Like magnets,
Repelling and attracting,
As the need arises.
Circling around one another,
Orbiting each other's perimeter,
Never staying long enough to understand
One another's elemental composition.

The female form is born with
A penchant for bending with the weather,
As pliable as good leather.
Eventually she acquires the necessities,
Stiletto heels,
A navel ring,
Push up bra,
Clanging bangles,
Eyeliner,
A virgin zone,

A customary moan,
Black teddy,
A bed,
A head.

The female form has a multitude of uses.
It has been used as a door knocker,
A bottle opener,
As a device to hold flashlights and lampshades,
A clock with a ticking belly,
A nutcracker,
A man basher.

It bears torches and extinguishes them,
Writes novels under male pseudonyms,
Lifts red and ribboned wreaths,
Raises glasses to cupboards,
Shines crystal,
Fills bathing suits.

Entire buildings rest on her granite stems.

It sells sports cars,
And beer,
Lipstick and malt liquor,
But the form does not merely sell,
It is sold.

The economics of continents rely on such a hearty and steady marketplace,

Razzle dazzle,

Cheap chattel,

And the money comes in,

Suitcase by leathered suitcase,

Slinking into the hands of men

Wearing expensive suits and ties,

Who ask, "You want to decrease the national debt don't, you?"

"Good. That's the spirit."

"That's my girl."

She's a profitable natural resource,

And luckily a renewable one,

Because those things wear out so quickly,

They don't make them like they used to,

Damned shoddy goods.

One and one is two,

Two and one is three,

"The more the merrier," they say.

But pleasure in the female form is not required.

They are made to create satisfaction,

Not experience it.

The body systems are all parts of a whole,
And color coordinated.
The circulatory route is red,
The lungs are blue,
Digestion is green (and frowned upon),
And the nerves are neon orange.
Naturally the skeleton is white,
Like a strand of pearls,
The reproductive system is optional,
Although most prefer a functioning one.
Afterall, what good is a car with no engine?

Each form arrives with a female brain,
The softest color of coral pink.
Handy.
Makes those things work.
Off without a hitch.
Right on time.
Stick pins in the brain and you get fascinating results.
Old pop songs,
New recipes,
Short circuits,
Bad dreams.
The female brain has two halves,
Biological companions,
Joined by a single dense cord,
A neural pathway from one side to the far other,

Sending sparks of electricity and information,
from one end of the form to the other and back,
Like a telephone line,
Like a conversation.

And she listens,
To both ends,
Back and forth,
Start to finish,
Every word,
She listens in.
Hearing every voice,
And every prayer.

Among so many needs,
The weeping of children,
And the chaos of our condition,
She loses her internal waypoint.
She forgets her true nature,
And she becomes something else,
Something outside herself.
Something that can keep this world turning.

The male brain,
Well,
That's a different matter.
The cord is thinner,

Only a hair's width,
The string connecting each half is transparent,
A pane of glass,
As thin as fog,
Space over here,
Time over there,
Music and grammar in that room,
Physics and photosynthesis in another,
In its own sealed compartment.

The right brain doesn't know what the left brain is doing,
Doesn't know it's even there at all,
Good for aiming though,
For hitting the target,
When you pull the trigger,

What is the target?
Who is the mark?
Who cares?
What's important is striking it,
Every single time.
That's the male brain for you.
No questions, only answers.
Objective.
Direct.
Precise.

That is why all the men are secretly sad.
And feel like orphans,
Desolate and disjoined,
Like driftwood,
Alone and unattached in the void.

"What void?" She asks,
"What are you talking about?"
"The void of the entire universe," he says.
She answers "Oh," and looks out the window,
Trying to hold onto the origin of his seclusion,
But it's no use.
She can't hold on,
Like trying to remember a dream after you wake.
There is too much in the air,
Too many voices,
To many things and tasks to complete,
Too many movies playing in her mind,
Too many children going hungry,
Too many wars raging outside,
So, she asks, "Would you like a beer? A piece of cake?"
And he grinds his teeth because she doesn't understand,
And he wanders off alone,
Lost in the millions of closets within his skull,
Searching blindly for the other half,
The twin who could complete him.

But after along while
Locked in solitude within his own dark rooms,
The instinctual urge within his lower brain begins to howl.
He grows lonely,
And the want begins to accumulate.
Something shines in the gloom,
Far ahead,
Through the locks and doors,
Hallways and rooms,
A vision of wholeness,
Ripeness,
Like a reddened berry,
Like an apple,
It blazes like a torch in the cold,
Like a watery, crying moon.

His reptilian mind whispers,
"Catch it.
Put it in a pumpkin,
A high tower."
His sharp sense of isolation subsides briefly,
Giving into the animal urges of his right brain,
The part in charge of action,
Of creation,
Of sex,
And momentarily he finds the other half,
His physiological companion,

The tiny space within his psyche that he'd long forgotten.

But it will not last.
It never does.
It can't.
How would it?

And soon enough he wonders (as she dresses herself by the bed),
"What target? Who is the mark? Who cares?"
Just hit the damn target.
Every time.
Every single time.

"The Marks Humans Leave"

If you ask me where I have been,
I must say,
Everywhere,
And,
Nowhere,

I must speak of the grounds darkened by the storms,
Of the river that forgotten,
Is destroyed,
I know only the things that remain here,
The sea left behind,
And children weeping.

Why so many regions,
So many islands,
So many countries?

Why do people leave,
Traveling thousands of miles,
And only arrive where they began?

If you ask me where I come from,
I must converse with broken things,
With plants bitter to excess,

With great hands that do not move,
With the cynicism of a thousand years,

Those that have crossed our paths
Leave marks,
Miles,
Memories.
And we learn to avoid the crow,
And the blacked winged mourner
That tearful face with its fingers against our throats,

And all the while
What falls down against the leaves,
And the light of a day gone by,
Is another day,
Both nourished
And devoured
By a sad and lonely blood.

"Declaration of War"

Phone line bomb blasts,
Copper wire and rubber sheath,
Thirty days to end a war,
Another lie wrapped in grief,

Something else is hiding here,
Some deep sadness to appease,
Forged from loneliness and neglect,
A debilitating disease,

Nothing left, but unseen prose,
Scribbled on a page,
So hungry there, I took a bite,
And traded my heart for a cage.

"Burning House"

When it is all said and done,
When damage has been totaled,
And there is nothing left of me to save,
I just want to be able to say,
That I loved you,
Not once,
Or twice,
But for as long as you allowed me,
Even when you weren't there,
Even when the house was burning,
Even when I didn't want to.

"Awakening"

And you tried to change
Didn't you?
Closed your mouth more,
Tried to be more pliable,
Prettier,
Less volatile,
Less awake,
But you can't make homes out of human beings,
Our mothers should have told us that.
You cannot eat the sins of men
And remain soft,
If he wants to leave, dear girl,
Let him go.

"Creation Unseen"

Her grace, she says, is all she has,
And that, she least displays
One art to recognize must be
Another art to praise,

The veins of flowers, delicate
Torched by fingers, are
The cousins of familiar vessels,
As "branch" to "jugular"

He will move on and she abides,
He'll conjugate her skill,
While she created and federates
Without a syllable

"Desolation"

The loneliest one dare not sound,
And would as soon surmise,
As in their grave go plummeting,
To ascertain its size.

The loneliness whose worst alarm
Is that itself should see,
And perish right before itself
From mere a scrutiny.

The loneliness will not lie still,
But skirts around in the dark,
With consciousness suspended,
Comes the risk of watermark.

My thickest fear is loneliness,
My soul the first to feel,
Its caverns and its corridors,
Illuminate or seal?

"War"

It was born in the blood,
This word.
This flaming contagion,
It grew in the dark and damp body,
Pulsating through veins,
Hardened by decision,
Blinded by the power of life and death,

Still and cold, it was born
From dead fathers,
From nomadic races,
From children who had no way to be called,
From cities made of granite,
That grow tired of their wretched names,

These cities walked,
Talked,
These cities arrived in business suits
And struck a deal,
That a new earth would merge with the old,
To sew their realities anew.

And so, this is the legacy,
This is the truth that connects us,
To the dead men,
The fallen sons,
The lost and sacred lands of nations,

The fluid sky still trembles
From that first word,
Formed in panic and in pain,

It rose from the manufactured shadows
Of powerful men,
And even now,
Thunder claps near it,
This world made pregnant too young
By negation,
By supply lines,
By the votes of men too old to lead,
By the death of a generation,

That verb "war"
Assumed all that potential,
Merging fire with flesh,
Existence with carnage,

That simple word,
Makes our planet bleed,

We pronounce
And
We reach
And
We are
Without speech,
What remains at the end of war.

"The Road"

She wasn't born herself,
But rather she found herself,
Over a long and treacherous road,

Over an arduous journey,
She gathered pieces of herself,
Stone by stone,
Brick by brick.

And while she traveled,
She realized,
That the more grueling the road became,
The more of herself she found.

"Home"

You elevate me.
You heighten abilities,
Sharpen my focus.
You make me levitate.

You steady me and stir me all at once.

I'm enamored,
And utterly strung out on you.

I want you to own every single broken,
Bruised,
Heavy,
And terrified portion of me.

You've captured me,
Mind and soul,
Bones to bones,

You feel like my childhood,
Like the first warm sip of coffee,
Like a perfect fall morning,
Like home.

"Certain Things"

I am not always sure,
How to get the poems to paper,
Without the hurt sticking helplessly
To words like "love" and "leave" and "stay"

But I know I miss your eyes
And the way they find me
In the early mornings,
When I wake next to you.

I know that in the smallest moments
Between us,
The spaces between our words,
The quiet moments
When we are simply breathing,
The soft dark minute before
We fall asleep,
That I love you.

"From Earth"

You stroke my soul.
I am half terror,
Half hope.

My thirst is made of fire
And want.
Urgency,
And peace.

The agony of not knowing you fully
Is palpable,
Weighing on me,
Like an appetite
I beg to satiate.

My hunger for you is from the earth,
From the soil of my beginnings and endings,
Dark and woody,
Deep and absolute.

Made in the USA
Columbia, SC
20 January 2024

a781b0be-d945-479e-9c62-4c569af0de33R05